A NOTE TO PARENTS

When your children are ready to "step into reading," giving them the right books is as crucial as giving them the right food to eat. **Step into Reading Books** present exciting stories and information reinforced with lively, colorful illustrations that make learning to read fun, satisfying, and worthwhile. They are priced so that acquiring an entire library of them is affordable. And they are beginning readers with a difference—they're written on five levels.

Early Step into Reading Books are designed for brand-new readers, with large type and only one or two lines of very simple text per page. **Step 1 Books** feature the same easy-to-read type as the Early Step into Reading Books, but with more words per page. **Step 2 Books** are both longer and slightly more difficult, while **Step 3 Books** introduce readers to paragraphs and fully developed plot lines. **Step 4 Books** offer exciting nonfiction for the increasingly independent reader.

The grade levels assigned to the five steps—preschool through kindergarten for the Early Books, preschool through grade 1 for Step 1, grades 1 through 3 for Step 2, grades 2 through 3 for Step 3, and grades 2 through 4 for Step 4—are intended only as guides. Some children move through all five steps very rapidly; others climb the steps over a period of several years. Either way, these books will help your child "step into reading" in style!

To Johnny Unitas,
with special thanks for his help with this manuscript.
And to my husband Rick, another all-time great—D. B.

Cover photographs: Duomo (J. Unitas); Allsport/Otto Greule (J. Elway); Allsport/Otto Greule (J. Montana); Allsport/Rick Stewart (S. Young); Allsport/Andy Lyons (D. Marino); Allsport/Al Bello (B. Favre).

Interior photographs: Duomo/Chris Trotman, p. 11; Duomo/Al Tielemans, p. 19; Duomo, p. 25, 46; Duomo/Steven Sutton, p. 31; Walter Iooss, Jr./*Sports Illustrated,* p. 39.

Library of Congress Cataloging-in-Publication Data
Bailer, Darice.
Touchdown! : great quarterbacks in football history / by Darice Bailer.
p. cm. — (Step into reading. A step 4 book)
Summary: Describes the achievements of six notable quarterbacks in the history of the National Football League, including John Elway, Brett Favre, and Joe Montana.
ISBN 0-679-88621-4 (trade) — ISBN 0-679-98621-9 (lib. bdg.)
1. Football players—United States—Biography—Juvenile literature.
2. Quarterback (Football)—Juvenile literature. [1. Football players. 2. Football—History.]
I. Title. II. Title: Great quarterbacks in football history. III. Series: Step into reading. Step 4 book.
GV939.A1B35 1999 796.332'092'273—dc21 [B] 98-51537

Printed in the United States of America 10 9 8 7 6 5 4 3 2 1
www.randomhouse.com/kids

STEP INTO READING, RANDOM HOUSE, and the Random House colophon are registered trademarks and the Step into Reading colophon is a trademark of Random House, Inc.

STEP INTO READING®

TOUCHDOWN!

Great Quarterbacks in Football History

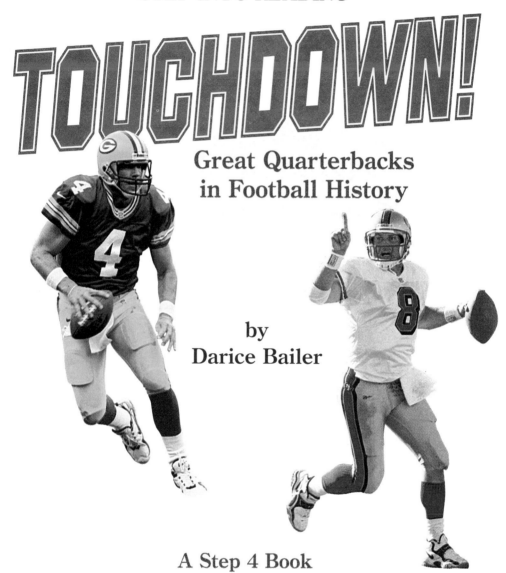

by
Darice Bailer

A Step 4 Book

Random House 🏠 New York

INTRODUCTION

Football's greatest quarterbacks were once kids like you. They tucked footballs under their arms and ran. They pretended their yards or streets were football fields. They threw passes to make-believe receivers. They dove into imaginary end zones, and at night, they slept beneath posters of their sports heroes.

And who *were* their heroes? Famous quarterbacks, of course! Who wouldn't dream of being a quarterback? He's the team leader, driving his team toward the goal line. Although a coach plans a team's plays, it is the quarterback who carries them out.

When his team gets the ball, the quarterback takes charge. The pressure is on him to win the game. Fans are screaming. Television cameras are rolling.

With his head up, the quarterback crouches behind the team's center. His palms form a cradle for the ball, waiting for the snap. His eyes are alert, watching the other side. He "reads" the defense, guessing his opponents' next moves.

Hike! The center snaps the ball between his legs. The quarterback grabs it and steps back as his teammates dash to carry out their assignments.

Three seconds—that's about all the time the quarterback's got to decide what to do with the ball. After that, the defenders tackle him. The quarterback can throw the ball, hand it to a teammate, or keep it and run.

The best quarterbacks find a way to win the most important games. When the pressure is hot, these quarterbacks are cool. They fake a pass—then hug the ball and scramble for a first down. Or they pretend to hand off the ball—then hurl a perfect, game-winning spiral.

Here are the stories of six great ones—champions who consistently came through in the clutch.

JOHN ELWAY

It's January 25, 1998. Super Bowl Sunday. The Green Bay Packers are the returning champs. Fans are betting they'll blow the Denver Broncos away. But this Super Bowl is no blow-out. Instead, it's a thriller! Green Bay scores on their first drive. Denver comes right back. At halftime, Denver leads. In the third quarter, the Packers kick a field goal. The game is now tied 17–17.

Time for Denver to take over. John Elway, their quarterback, trots onto the field. At 37, John's one of the oldest quarterbacks still playing. But he's also one of the best. He's thrown for more yards than everyone in football history except Miami's Dan Marino.

He's won the most games. Yet he's played in the Super Bowl three times and lost each game.

John's always wanted a Super Bowl ring. Today may be his last shot. He's thinking about retiring. If he wins, he retires a champion. If he loses, people will remember his 0–4 record in football's biggest game.

Many fans are rooting for John today, but none more than his dad.

Mr. Elway coached football at high school and later at college level. When John was in elementary school, Mr. Elway would toss the football around with him in a field near their Missoula, Montana, home.

At 11 years old, John played running back in his first organized football game. Because of his coaching job, Mr. Elway couldn't make it until halftime. By then, John had already run for four touchdowns! Mr.

Elway made sure to show up on time for John's *next* game.

John played quarterback in high school. He became the best football player his father had ever seen.

In high school and college, John was a football star. He set national college records at Stanford University in California. He also played right field for the baseball team. He threw the ball so hard that the New York Yankees recruited him! Before graduating from college, John played six weeks for the Yankees' minor league team.

In the 1983 college football draft, John was picked first. The Yankees wanted to sign him, but John opted for football. He signed on with the Denver Broncos instead. He became famous for his strong right arm. John hurled the ball with such force that it whistled across the field. Once, the tip of his ball left an X-shaped mark on a receiver's chest!

Even more amazing were John's last-minute heroics. Many times, when the Broncos fell behind in the fourth quarter, John led them back to tie the game or win. He did it 41 times, more than any other professional quarterback.

Now John wants to make the biggest comeback of his career—from three-time loser to Super Bowl champ.

The Broncos have the ball at their own eight-yard line, 92 yards away from the end zone. In ten plays, John drives his team forward 80 yards. Now Denver has the ball at the Green Bay 12 and it's third down. John needs six more yards for a first down.

Hike! John drops back to pass. He scans the field. None of his receivers are free.

An excellent runner, John darts straight ahead. He cuts right to avoid a tackle. *Blocked!* One of the Packers' best defensive

players is there. His name is LeRoy Butler.
LeRoy lowers his head to butt into John.

John can't let LeRoy stop him now. John
dives over him, trying to reach the first-

down marker. LeRoy smashes into him before his body clears. Another Packer rams him as he hits the ground.

John's body aches, but his heart is filled with joy. He gained eight yards—enough for a critical first down—and reached the four-yard line! John's teammates are charged up and ready to keep going. And two plays later, they score!

The Packers come back to tie the game, but not for long. With one minute and 45 seconds left in the game, the Broncos score again.

Now it's the Packers' ball. John paces. If only his team can hold the lead. With 28 seconds left, Packers' quarterback Brett Favre tries to pass, but it's swatted down. The Packer drive—and game—is over!

Instead of the expected Green Bay blow-out, it's a 31–24 Denver upset! John has his long-denied Super Bowl victory at last!

The Broncos hoist John onto their shoulders and carry him across the field. Fireworks explode in the sky. *"El-way! El-way!"* the crowd chants.

John climbs up the stairs to an awards platform. The Broncos' team president lifts up the silver trophy. "This one's for John!" he says.

In the locker room, John's son Jack asks to see his dad's Super Bowl ring. John laughs—the ring hasn't been made yet.

But John's career *is* made. He will win one more Super Bowl before retiring in 1999.

When John was in fifth grade:

John hated to lose—at *any* game! Once, during a basketball game, John thought his team wasn't trying hard enough. That made him mad. He yelled at the other kids.

After the game, John's father pulled him

aside. You shouldn't treat people that way, said Mr. Elway. They deserve more respect.

As for John's athletic talent and versatility, that was well respected. He made so many baskets that one coach named him "Shotgun"!

BRETT FAVRE

Super Bowl Sunday, January 26, 1997. Thousands of Green Bay Packer fans jam the New Orleans Superdome. *"Go, Brett, go!"* they scream.

Brett Favre is the Packers' young quarterback. He's a fun-loving guy. Cracking jokes and playing pranks are two of his favorite things.

Packer fans are called cheeseheads. The team plays in Wisconsin—the state that makes most of our nation's cheese. Some fans wear large wedges of fake cheese on their heads.

The cheeseheads are charged up to beat the New England Patriots. Brett is too.

*   *   *

Brett grew up just an hour's drive from the Superdome, in a small Mississippi town. He was a stubborn kid. When he made up his mind to do something, he did it. And Brett made up his mind to win football games.

Even in elementary school, Brett could throw farther than the older kids. In fifth grade, he told his coach he wanted to play quarterback. Next game, Brett did. He ran for two touchdowns and threw for a third.

In high school, Brett's father was his coach. After Friday night games, Brett didn't party. He did pushups and situps instead. By tenth grade, Brett had decided he would play in the pros.

He had the drive to make it—and he was a leader, to boot. In college, Brett would tell his teammates, "Let's whip these guys." And they did, winning many important games.

Brett was 22 when he joined the Packers

in 1992. At first, he had trouble learning all the offensive plays. He threw so many interceptions, he almost lost his starting job.

But Brett wasn't about to let someone else take over. He'd show everyone he could throw better.

He listened to tips from his coach, Mike Holmgren. That helped. In four seasons, Brett threw 147 touchdowns. Only Dan Marino threw more. In 1995 and 1996, Brett was named MVP (Most Valuable Player) of the league.

But Brett wanted another title. Super Bowl Champ.

Inside the Superdome, the Patriots receive the ball first. They fail to score.

Brett takes over. Before his second play, Brett studies how the Patriots line up. He has a feeling they'll rush him in an all-out blitz. *Good.* With the Patriots ganging up on him, Brett's receivers will be wide open downfield. At the last minute, Brett shouts for receiver Andre Rison to run deep.

The ball is snapped. The Patriot rush is fierce, but Brett stays cool. He whips the ball down the middle of the field. Brett's pass is right on target. Andre catches it on the run and scores! The Packers lead 7–0. Brett clenches his fist and shouts for joy.

In the second quarter, Brett feels another blitz coming. At the line of scrimmage, Brett calls for his blockers to protect him. He grabs the snap and scrambles to pass. He looks downfield and spots Antonio Freeman, a wide receiver. Brett is famous for scrambling, finding the open man, and making big plays on the spur of the moment. He's also famous for his quick release. Before the Patriots can bring him down, Brett flings a pass. Antonio grabs it and runs 81 yards. *Touchdown, Packers!* The cheeseheads roar!

The Packers hang on to their lead. Toward the end of the game, Brett points his index finger up to the sky. With the 35–21 victory, the Packers are number one— and so is he.

Next season, Brett makes up his mind to win a *third* straight MVP award—and he does!

Now Brett's goal is to become the best quarterback of all time. No doubt about it—he'll work hard to achieve that goal, too.

When Brett was seven:

Brett and his two brothers would hose down their yard. Then they'd put on their pads and play football. Tackling each other in the sloppy mud was fun!

The boys had to be careful playing football near their house, though. There were alligators living in a murky river running through their front yard.

One day, the family's dog disappeared. Brett's father said that an alligator ate it!

DAN MARINO

January 6, 1985. Miami Dolphins' quarterback Dan Marino is 23. He graduated from college less than two years ago. Yet he has already taken his team to the American Football Conference Championship.

The Dolphins are playing the Pittsburgh Steelers in the Orange Bowl. At stake— a trip to the Super Bowl. Playing there is every quarterback's dream...and it's been Dan's dream ever since he was a boy.

Dan grew up in Pittsburgh on a street with houses built close together. The yards were too small to play in, so neighborhood kids played in the street or in nearby parks or fields. Games were tough and competitive.

Dan's father taught him how to throw quickly. He told Dan to start with the ball next to his ear and snap it forward with his wrist. That way, he could throw without wasting time or motion.

Dan practiced throwing at telephone poles and stop signs. "Then I'd pick up the ball and do it again," he said. Dan threw the ball faster and farther than any other kid around. At ten, he knew he wanted to play professional football.

In high school, Dan broke the school passing records. He also excelled at baseball. He was a superb pitcher, winning 25 games in a row! He was so good that the Kansas City Royals baseball team drafted him!

But Dan cared more about football than baseball. And he wanted to play for the University of Pittsburgh—just five blocks from his house.

Early on, Pittsburgh Panthers' coach Jackie Sherrill gave Dan some advice. "Whatever you do, don't ever let any coach tell you how to throw a football or change anything you're doing."

It was some of the best advice Dan ever received. Dan went on to lead the Panthers to four straight bowl games. He also broke several school passing records.

After college, in 1983, Dan began playing for the Miami Dolphins. He played amazingly well for a rookie.

Dan threw balls with just the right touch so that they could be caught easily. His 58 percent completion rate set an NFL rookie record. He was asked to play in the Pro Bowl with the league's best players—the first rookie quarterback ever to start in that game.

The following season, Dan's numbers topped the record charts—362 passes for 5,084 yards and 48 touchdowns.

*   *   *

At the American Football Conference Championship, kids hang over the railings inside the Orange Bowl. They wear Dan's number and scream his name as he runs onto the field.

After taking his first snap, Dan looks downfield. His eyes focus on receiver Mark Clayton.

The Steelers try to sack Dan before he can get off a pass, but they're too slow. Before they lay a hand on him, Dan whips the ball to Mark. The tip of the football strikes him in the chest. *Bull's-eye!* Mark runs 40 yards to score. The extra-point kick is good, and the Dolphins lead 7–0.

Dan *looks* like a winner tonight! After each snap, he grabs the ball and spots the open man. He throws three more touchdowns before the game ends. The Steelers don't sack him once! Miami wins 45–28.

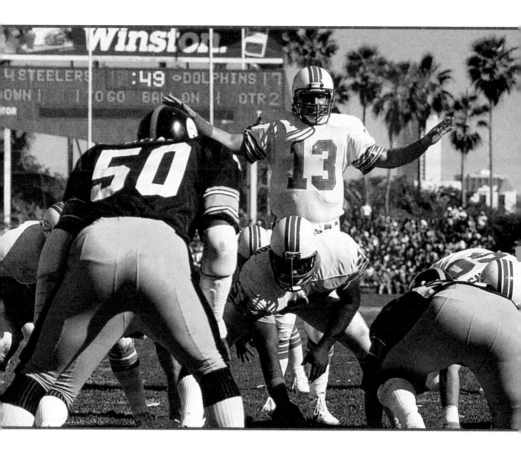

Dan's four touchdowns and 421 passing yards set AFC Championship records.

"If he stays healthy, he'll rewrite the NFL record books," predicts one Steeler. And that's just what Dan does.

On November 26, 1995, against Indianapolis, Dan threw his 343rd touchdown pass. In 75 years, no NFL quarterback had ever thrown that many touchdowns in his career. It is one of over two dozen records Dan has set during his career.

As fans stood and cheered, Dan retrieved the record-setting ball. He handed it to a man from the Pro Football Hall of Fame. It would be put on display at the Hall of Fame Museum in Canton, Ohio. No doubt *Dan's* a future Hall of Famer, too!

When Dan was a young boy:

Dan received his first number-13 uniform. His Little League baseball coach handed it to him. Dan's coach was his dad. Mr. Marino gave Dan number 13 because no other kid would wear it!

The other kids thought 13 was an unlucky number. Not Dan. He proved that it was a *lucky* number for him. Dan went on to wear a 13 in college and in the pros, too!

JOE MONTANA

Sunday, January 22, 1989. It's the San Francisco 49ers versus the Cincinnati Bengals at the Super Bowl. The Bengals lead 16–13. Three minutes and ten seconds remain in the game.

Joe Montana snaps on his helmet and trots onto the field. Joe is San Francisco's quarterback, and the 49ers have the ball. Fans scream for Joe to take their team to victory.

Joe usually plays his best in the fourth quarter. Will the same hold true today? Can Joe live up to his nickname, the "Comeback Kid"?

*　　*　　*

Joe was born on June 11, 1956, in a small town in western Pennsylvania. He lived 30 miles from Pittsburgh. The area is known for its coal mines, steel mills, and, surprisingly, quarterbacks! Many famous quarterbacks grew up here: Dan Marino, Jim Kelly of the Buffalo Bills, Joe Namath of the New York Jets, and Johnny Unitas of the Baltimore Colts.

As soon as Joe could walk, his father taught him to throw. Before Joe was ten, his father hung a tire on a rope from a tree branch. He would swing the tire back and forth, and Joe would sling the football through the moving tire.

This taught Joe how to hurl the ball at just the right moment. He also learned to hit a moving target. Joe developed a strong and accurate arm.

Yet when Joe was ten years old, he

almost gave up football! During the middle of peewee football season, he told his dad he wanted to quit. He wanted to join the Cub Scouts.

"I don't want you to quit something you've started," Joe's father said. "You finish the season, and then you can quit football." Luckily, by the time football season ended, Joe had forgotten all about the Cub Scouts.

In high school, Joe joined the football team. He was so skinny, his coach called him "Joe Banana."

In college, Joe played for Notre Dame University. Joe is famous for his last college game. At the 1979 Cotton Bowl, Notre Dame played the University of Houston. It was a bitterly cold day.

Joe was sick with the flu and wasn't playing well. At halftime, Houston led 20–12. Joe shivered in the locker room. "I felt like I was sitting in a bucket of ice," Joe said. He sat out most of the third quarter, drinking chicken soup to keep warm. Meanwhile, out on the field, Notre Dame fell further behind.

With eight minutes left, Notre Dame trailed 34–12. It was then that the team doctor gave Joe the go-ahead to play.

Joe went to work. Notre Dame scored on a blocked punt, and Joe passed to a receiver in the end zone for a two-point conversion. Then Joe ran for a touchdown and passed for *another* two-point conversion. *Whoa!* Notre Dame gained 16 points for a 34–28 game.

In the final moment, Notre Dame got the ball again and headed back toward the Houston end zone. With only two seconds left, Joe huddled with his teammates at the Houston eight-yard line. Could Joe engineer yet *another* touchdown? "Let's do it," Joe said.

Joe cut right and threw. A Notre Dame receiver dove for the ball. He caught it in the end zone to tie the game as time ran out. With the extra-point kick, Notre Dame won 35–34. It was unbelievable.

*   *   *

At the Super Bowl, the "Comeback Kid" gets ready.

The Bengals are ahead 16–13, and the ball rests on San Francisco's eight-yard line. The 49ers must move the ball almost the length of the field to win.

"The 49ers have a long way to go!" says a television announcer.

Cincinnati fans don't think Joe has enough time. "We've got 'em now!" a Cincinnati player screams.

But this Bengal player has forgotten Joe's nickname. The Bengals have to keep Joe from launching a big drive. "[Give it] all you got on defense!" the Cincinnati coach hollers at his team.

Joe throws one pinpoint pass after another. The 49ers creep closer to the goal line. "One of the all-time greats is doing his thing again," a commentator remarks.

To save time, Joe calls two plays at once.

He screams to be heard over the roar of the crowd. Joe yells so loud that he feels dizzy.

Soon, just 39 seconds remain. The 'Niners are ten yards from the goal line and victory. Joe looks for receiver John Taylor as John races toward the end zone.

With just 34 seconds left, John grabs Joe's pass. *Touchdown!* With the extra-point kick, San Francisco takes a 20–16 lead and soon wins.

Joe grins and raises his helmet to the crowd. His touchdown will be remembered as "the Drive."

Next season, Joe takes the 49ers back to the Super Bowl. And he picks up his *fourth* Super Bowl ring.

In 1993, Joe joins the Kansas City Chiefs. In 1995, he retires as one of the greatest quarterbacks of all time.

When Joe was your age:

Joe couldn't wait for his dad to come home from work to play with him. He sat by the front door, holding a ball in his hands. Each night, the two threw baseballs and footballs back and forth in the yard.

Joe's grandfather saw that his grandson had talent. He told Joe's grandmother that Joe was going to be a great athlete one day. His observation proved true!

JOHNNY UNITAS

December 28, 1958. It's the National Football League Championship between the Baltimore Colts and the New York Giants.

The game is played at New York's Yankee Stadium. With just seven seconds left, the Colts kick a field goal. The game is tied 17–17.

The crowd grows quiet as the clock runs out. No professional football game has *ever* ended in a tie.

The referees confer and decide to continue the game to declare a winner. It will be the first NFL game to go into sudden-death overtime. Whoever scores first will be the new NFL champion.

The Giants win a coin toss. They choose to receive the ball. But they fail to score.

Johnny Unitas, the Baltimore quarterback, huddles with his team. He's a tall, skinny guy with a blond crew cut. The pressure to win doesn't make him nervous. People say he has ice water running through his veins, he's that cool.

Johnny is matter-of-fact in the huddle. "We're going to take the ball, and we're going to go right down and score this time," he says.

Johnny lines up, planting his black cleats in the ground. Three years ago, he couldn't get a job in pro football. Coaches didn't think he was any good.

Today they will think otherwise.

Johnny was born on May 7, 1933, in Pittsburgh, Pennsylvania. When Johnny was five, his father died of pneumonia.

Johnny was the second youngest of four children. His mother went to work to earn money for the family. With his father gone and his mother working, Johnny took care of himself. He learned to make decisions on his own.

Johnny and an older brother took over their father's coal-delivery business. Johnny built up his muscles shoveling coal.

Johnny's high school football coach noticed his strong throwing arm and picked him to be quarterback. He taught Johnny to map out his plays. "You're like a coach on the field," his coach told him. Johnny didn't forget those words.

In college, Johnny completed 11 of his first 12 passes in his first game. He set 15 school records. His dream was to play in the pros.

In 1955, the Pittsburgh Steelers drafted Johnny. Before training camp ended, the

Steeler coaches cut him from the team. They didn't think Johnny could remember all the plays.

Johnny could have given up, but he didn't. He played for a semipro team. But he kept dreaming of the real thing—playing in the National Football League. The next year, in 1956, the Colts hired him. Johnny would prove to the Colts that they made a smart choice.

The 1958 NFL Championship is Johnny's chance. It's sudden-death overtime, and the ball's at the Colts' 20-yard line. But when he tries to make his first pass, Johnny is sacked.

He gets right up. He won't let the other team think that they've hurt him.

Johnny completes his next two passes. On the next play, Johnny prepares to make his third. It's fourth down with eight yards

to go. Receiver Raymond Berry is open, but he's only five yards beyond the line of scrimmage. That's three yards short of a first down.

Even as his opponents rush at him, Johnny stays cool. He'll show the Giants he's not afraid of them. Johnny stands still, motioning to Ray with his hands. He tells him to keep going. Ray needs to catch Johnny's pass a little farther downfield.

A split second before he's knocked down

by his opponents, Johnny releases the ball. Ray nabs it in first-down territory—at the Giants' 1.

In 12 plays, Johnny moves the Colts 79 yards. There's one yard to go to the goal line.

Three plays later, Johnny hands the ball to a fullback, who charges into the end zone. The Colts win 23–17.

"The Colts are the world champions!" yells a TV announcer.

Fans rush onto the field. Johnny is named MVP. People say that this is the greatest football game ever played.

The next year, the Colts and Johnny are NFL champs again. And in 1971, they win Super Bowl V.

Johnny set many records before he retired in 1973. No wonder he opened a restaurant called The Golden Arm.

When Johnny was your age:

Johnny walked two miles to school and back each day. He even walked home for lunch. There was no school bus for him to ride.

After school, Johnny liked to join eight or nine kids in the neighborhood and play. "We played everything," Johnny said.

As a kid, Johnny couldn't pretend he was a pro football player—he didn't know any! "Football wasn't that big at that time," Johnny explained. "I couldn't tell you who was on the team in those days."

It wasn't until Johnny was an adult, in 1958, that the first football game was televised. It was the NFL Championship—Johnny's big game!

STEVE YOUNG

Super Bowl Sunday. January 29, 1995. Miami, Florida.

The San Francisco 49er players are introduced before the kickoff. Steve Young is the 49ers' quarterback. When Steve hears his name announced, his face lights up. This is his dream come true.

It's Steve's chance to prove that he can win the Super Bowl—just like Joe Montana. Joe quarterbacked the team before Steve and won four Super Bowls.

The San Francisco fans loved Joe. When he left in 1993 and Steve took over, they complained that Steve wasn't nearly as good. Steve had lost games that kept San Francisco out of the Super Bowl.

But not this year. The 49ers are back at the Super Bowl, facing the tough San Diego Chargers. Steve runs onto the field with his fist held high.

At his first college football practice, nobody would have thought Steve was Super Bowl material. Steve attended Brigham Young University in Utah. Brigham Young had one of the best passing games in the country. Unfortunately, Steve couldn't throw the ball well at all.

At his first BYU practice, Steve tried to complete a pass, but he tripped over his own feet and fell. The other players laughed. Steve wanted to quit and go home. "You can quit, but you can't come home," his dad said.

Jim McMahon was BYU's starting quarterback. Jim set 72 National Collegiate Athletic Association (NCAA) records. When Jim graduated, he joined the Chicago Bears.

At BYU, Steve watched Jim throw and

copied his style. He practiced throwing each day and began to improve.

When Jim graduated, Steve took over as starting quarterback. Over the next two years, Steve tied and/or set 13 NCAA records. During his senior year, he was the runner-up for the Heisman Trophy—the award that is given to the nation's best college football player.

Steve graduated from BYU in 1984. He then played for the Los Angeles Express, a team that no longer exists. In 1985 and 1986, he played for the Tampa Bay Buccaneers. He threw more interceptions than touchdowns. In 1987, the Buccaneers traded him to the 49ers. San Francisco wanted a backup for Joe Montana.

As a backup quarterback, Steve didn't play much. But he had plenty of time to watch Joe play. Steve learned a lot from watching him. When Joe got injured, Steve stepped in. The more Steve played, the more he learned.

Steve began to sense where his receivers would be on the field. He relaxed and threw the ball better. He completed more passes and won more games. From 1991 to 1994, Steve led the National Football League in passing.

Now he has taken the 49ers to the Super Bowl. This is the most important game of his career!

Steve usually feels nervous before big games. He is often afraid he will let his team down. But not today. Today he feels calm.

Steve completes his first pass and moves the 49ers 11 yards. On his second play, he hands off the ball. The 'Niners pick up seven more yards. On his third play, Steve drops back and searches the field for Jerry Rice—the 49ers' best receiver.

Steve sees Jerry running toward the end zone. Steve knows he must throw quickly before he is sacked. He flings a bomb down the middle of the field.

Jerry reaches up and snags it. He runs 44 yards to the end zone.

Touchdown, 49ers! No quarterback has ever thrown a Super Bowl touchdown so early in the game—after only one minute and 24 seconds.

Three minutes later, Steve hurls another touchdown to running back Ricky Watters. The 49ers now lead 14–0.

Steve throws two more touchdowns before halftime, and two more after. No quarterback has ever thrown *six* touchdowns in a Super Bowl. Not even the great Joe Montana!

San Diego finds Steve tough to defend against. If the Chargers try to block his running, he passes. If the Chargers try to block his passing, he runs. Steve gains 49 rushing yards, more than any running back in the game!

The 49ers win their fifth Super Bowl, 49–26. Steve holds his helmet up to the crowd. This is one of the happiest moments of his life.

Steve is chosen as the game's MVP. In the locker room, there are tears in his eyes. He has proved that he is a winner. Just like Joe Montana!

When Steve was in junior high school:

Steve received his first number-eight jersey at junior high school football practice. At first, he was disappointed. "This isn't much of a number," Steve thought, looking at his uniform. "No one wears eight. Only dummies wear eight."

But Steve was wrong. Not only would Steve win the Super Bowl wearing number eight, but Troy Aikman of the Dallas Cowboys has won three Super Bowls wearing number eight, too!